RADIATION:

Waves and Particles/
Benefits and Risks

LAURENCE PRINGLE

ENSLOW PUBLISHERS
Bloy Street and Ramsey Avenue
Box 777
Hillside, New Jersey 07205

[c1983]

Library of Congress Cataloging in Publication Data:

Pringle, Laurence P.
  Radiation: waves & particles.

  Bibliography: p.
  Includes index.
  1. Radiation. I. Title.
QC795.P74   1983   539.2   82-16721
ISBN 0-89490-054-4 ✔

Printed in the United States of America

10 9 8 7 6 5 4 3 2 1

Photo Credits:
American Cancer Society, pp. 27, 29, 47; Argonne National Laboratory, p. 45; Brookhaven National Laboratory, pp. 40, 48, 49; Environmental Protection Agency, cover (lower left), p. 4; Federal Aviation Administration, p. 56; Health Sciences Markets Division, Eastman Kodak Company, Rochester, New York, cover (lower right), pp. 9, 24, 26; Los Alamos Scientific Laboratory, pp. 14, 18; Oak Ridge National Laboratory, p. 39; courtesy of Owens-Corning Fiberglass Corporation, p. 8; Picker International, Inc., p. 30, 31; Laurence Pringle, cover (upper right), pp. 6, 15, 36; U.S. Air Force, p. 18; U.S. Army, p. 43; U.S. Department of Energy, Grand Junction Office, pp. 38, 46; U.S. Food and Drug Administration, p. 52; U.S.Navy, p. 53; United Nations, photo by Yosuke Yamahata, p. 20.

Contents

The Range of Radiation

Radiation feels good on a spring day. The warmth of sunshine is a form of radiation we take for granted, but it is only part of the radiation we receive, day and night.

Some comes from the natural environment, some from human activities and devices. Some radiation can harm cells in our bodies and can kill people. The same kind of radiation can be used to detect or cure disease. Still, for many people, radiation is a scary word. There is growing concern about the dangers of certain kinds, and how to avoid them. So it is important to learn about the radiation in our lives.

Radiation is energy in motion. Some forms of radiation can be thought of as moving particles. The particles are tiny bits of matter, including protons, neutrons, and electrons, which make up atoms. Such particles make up most of the dangerous radiation that is emitted from wastes of nuclear power plants.

Other forms of radiation move as waves. Heat, light, X-rays, and radio waves are examples of radiation that travel as waves. It is called electromagnetic radiation because the waves consist of disturbances in the electric and magnetic fields that are all around us.

People are exposed to different kinds of radiation everywhere, from the sun and other stars, from machines, and from their surroundings.

Of all electromagnetic radiation, the kind we know best is visible light. As you read these words, radiation from an electric light or the sun is reflected from the page to your eyes. As you look around a room or outdoors you see different colors of light reflected. All of this visible light, as well as other electromagnetic radiation, travels at the same speed—186,282 miles a second (or 299,782 kilometers a second). The sunlight around you *now* left the sun about eight minutes ago.

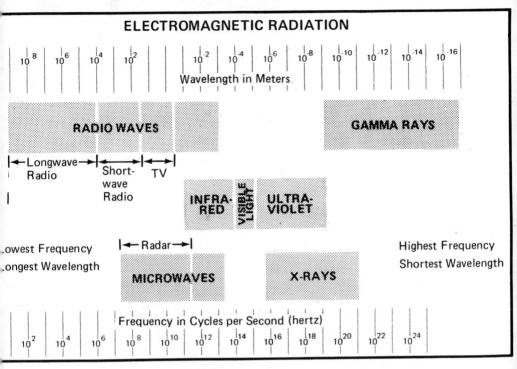

Two different kinds of radiation, X-rays and gamma rays for example, may have identical wavelengths and frequencies.

The chart on this page shows the full range of electromagnetic radiation. As you can see, visible light takes up only a narrow band near the middle. Although all of these kinds of radiation travel at the same speed, they differ in wavelength (the distance between wave peaks) and in frequency (the number of vibrations per second). Frequency is measured in cycles per second, also expressed as hertz—after the German scientist, Heinrich R. Hertz, who first produced and detected radio waves.

Frequency and Wavelength

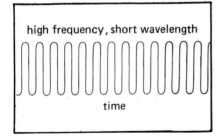

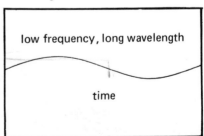

Some radio waves measure more than six miles (96 kilometers) between crests of their waves. Waves that are very long have very low frequencies. In shortwave radio—the kind used by police and by amateur "ham" radio operators—wavelengths are actually quite long; they're called shortwave only because they are among the shortest of *radio* waves. Such wavelengths were used in the first practical application of radio—communication between ships in the early 1900's. Radio messages helped the rescue of hundreds of people after the sinking of the passenger ship *Titanic* in 1912.

The "10X" on this radio dial (lower right) indicates that the AM frequency numbers are actually ten times greater than shown. They range from 535 to 1605 kilohertz.

The radio waves most familiar to people are those that bring us music, news, and other programs. Almost everyone has a favorite station and knows its number on the radio dial, usually without knowing what the number means. Each station is assigned a specific frequency in which to broadcast. Those of AM radio range from 535 to 1605 kilohertz. Wavelengths at those frequencies are hundreds of meters long. FM broadcasts are in the range of 88 to 108 megahertz. An FM radio station broadcasting at 99 megahertz—99 on the radio dial—transmits radio waves that are just a few meters long.

During World War II, an English scientist was asked whether radio waves could be used as a "death ray" against German bombers. They could not, but the scientist developed a way to detect and locate approaching aircraft by using reflected radio waves. The word *radar* is based on the four words that describe its function: *r*adio *d*etection *a*nd *r*anging.

Eventually, the short radio wavelengths used in radar were given their own name: microwaves. Many other uses have been found for them. They relay telephone and television signals over long distances and citizens band (CB) radio conversations over short distances. Microwaves transmit signals to open garage doors automatically and also cook food in special ovens.

Microwave and radio wavelengths overlap somewhat with infrared radiation. It was discovered in 1800 by an English astronomer, Sir William Herschel. He let a beam of sunlight shine through a glass prism so that the light was separated into its spectrum, or rainbow, of colors. He placed thermometers where the various colors appeared and discovered that red light made the temperature rise the most. Then he put a thermometer beyond the red end of the spectrum, where no light was visible. The temperature rose highest of all there.

Herschel concluded that the sun emits invisible heat radiation. Later he found that the same invisible radiation comes from hot coals in a fireplace. This radiation is called infrared, since *infra* means below and this radiation has a lower frequency than visible red light. Infrared radiation is emitted by virtually every warm substance or object on earth—rocks, water, buildings, and living things, including your own body.

Without infrared and visible radiation the earth would be a cold and barren place. The energy of visible light is converted into food energy by green plants, upon which all animals depend. Almost all energy sources, including wood, coal, oil, and gasoline, represent power from the sun, some of which was converted to plant energy millions of years ago. Even wind and water power come from the sun, since solar radiation creates the earth's weather.

Infrared and visible light are the only electromagnetic radiation we normally see or feel. Visible radiation is energetic enough to cause the chemical changes in normal photographic film that make photography possible. Special infrared film has

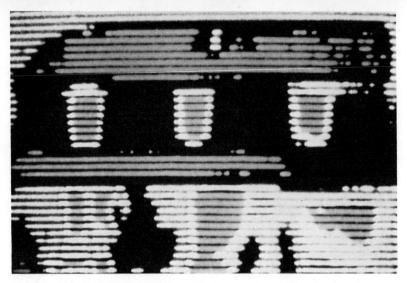

An infrared photograph of a house reveals where loss of infrared (heat) radiation is greatest.

also been devised to photograph heat radiation. With this film, pictures can be taken of the exterior of homes to locate places where heat escapes. Then insulation can be added or other steps taken to reduce energy loss.

Among the colors of visible light, reds have the longest wavelengths—33,000 waves cover an inch. Blues and violets, at the opposite end of the spectrum, have shorter wavelengths. There are about 66,000 violet waves in an inch. Just beyond the last visible violet light lies ultraviolet radiation. The Latin word *ultra* means beyond.

Ultraviolet radiation was discovered in the early 1800's by the German physicist Johann Ritter. Like Sir William Herschel, he passed a beam of sunlight through a prism, creating a spectrum of colored light. Then he put a white compound, silver chloride—which turns black when exposed to radiation— beyond the violet light of the spectrum. No light seemed to be shining there, yet the silver chloride turned black, indicating ultraviolet radiation.

Just as there is a range of wavelengths among visible light radiation, there is a range of ultraviolet waves. The shortest wavelengths have great energy and penetrating power. These waves are energetic enough to damage cells in human skin. This happens to millions of people each year. We call it sunburn. People use lotions and creams to block the most energetic ultraviolet radiation from reaching their skin and to allow less energetic ultraviolet rays through. The longer wavelengths are called tanning rays, but they too can sometimes damage skin. Too much ultraviolet radiation causes the skin to age prematurely and may cause skin cancer.

A more harmful form of radiation is called ionizing radiation. While ultraviolet rays are strong enough to "excite" electrons of atoms, they cannot knock them loose. Some radiation is powerful enough to rip electrons from atoms, leaving them with a positive electrical charge, or to add electrons, leaving them with a negative charge. Such atoms are called ions, and radiation that creates ions is called ionizing radiation. This powerful energy can damage cells in humans and other living things. Ionizing radiation is the source of most of today's concern about the dangers of radiation and is the main subject of this book.

X-rays have the power to create ions. X-ray wavelengths are even shorter than those of ultraviolet light. They were discovered and named by German physicist Wilhelm Roentgen in 1895. X-rays are given off naturally by the sun, but the earth's atmosphere keeps them from reaching its surface. This is fortunate, because the most energetic X-rays have great penetrating power. They pass easily through human flesh and can damage or kill cells.

X-ray photographs of a chambered nautilus (left) and a turtle.

 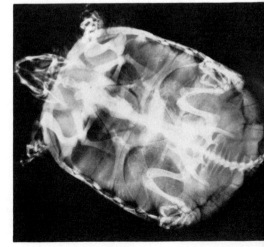

Most of the X-rays on earth come from machines, and their wavelength depends on the voltage of electricity used to produce them—the higher the voltage, the shorter the wavelength and the greater the penetrating power of the radiation. X-rays have many uses in industry and in medicine. Though they pass easily through flesh and tissues, they are mostly stopped by denser parts such as teeth and bones. So X-rays aimed at part of a person reveal interior details on a sheet of X-ray-sensitive film placed behind the person. Black areas on an X-ray film show where radiation passed through easily, gray areas where some was blocked, and white areas where they were stopped by dense objects. Such details as bullets, bone fractures, and tooth cavities can be revealed in this way.

Only one kind of electromagnetic radiation is more powerful than X-rays. Some gamma rays have even shorter wavelengths, though most gamma rays differ from X-rays only in the way they are produced. X-rays are usually emitted from machines, though some, like gamma rays, are given off as certain kinds of atomic nuclei break down or decay.

Unstable forms of elements that give off energy in this way are called radioactive isotopes. Uranium is the best known of about 50 elements that are naturally radioactive. Gamma rays come from the core, or nucleus, of the atoms of radioactive isotopes. They are the most energetic and most penetrating of all electromagnetic radiation.

gamma rays are the most powerful kind of electromagnetic radiation

alpha particles consist of two protons and two neutrons which behave like a single particle

beta particles are high-speed electrons

Radiation that travels as particles, not waves, is also emitted by radioactive atoms. These fragments of atoms all have the power to knock other atoms apart, creating ions and releasing energy, so they too may harm living things. The particles include alpha rays, which have a positive electrical charge and lose large amounts of energy quickly. A sheet or two of paper will stop alpha rays. Beta rays are high-speed electrons that travel almost as fast as the speed of light and can penetrate about a half-inch (13 millimeters) of wood. Both alpha and beta radiation occur naturally, while another kind of ionizing particle—the neutron—is produced mainly in nuclear reactors.

Finally, there is one other kind of radiation: cosmic rays. They come mostly from the sun and from more distant stars, and are primarily protons. As these particles enter the atmosphere they interact with atoms in the air to produce other kinds of particles, which may decay or interact further. As a result of these changes, the cosmic radiation that actually reaches the earth's surface includes gamma rays and electrons.

Cosmic rays rain down upon us. They pass right through our bodies and through other living things. They have been detected hundreds of feet underground. Like most radiation, however, they are invisible, unfelt, and unnoticed.

It's Only Natural 2

Though we acknowledge our dependence on the energy and warmth of the sun, we usually ignore the other kinds of radiation that are also part of our environment. Every day we are bombarded by this natural or background radiation. The amount that people receive depends partly on where they live and partly on their activities.

A common unit for measuring exposure to radiation is called the rem. It stands for "*r*oentgen *e*quivalent *m*an," and refers to the amount of radiation needed to produce a particular amount of damage in living tissue. Another unit of radiation exposure is the rad, named from the term "*r*adiation *a*bsorbed *d*ose." It is a measure of the radiation that is actually absorbed by tissues and bones, from all kinds of ionizing radiation. For X-rays, beta rays, and gamma rays, rads and rems are equal.

Not all types of ionizing radiation cause the same amount of tissue damage. In X-rays, beta rays, and gamma rays, ten rads of exposure equals about ten rems of damage. With alpha rays, however, ten rads of exposure will yield about a hundred rems of damage. The alpha particle causes more damage because it moves slowly and causes many more ionizations along its path than a speedy beta particle. Although alpha rays cannot penetrate the skin, if they get into the body they can cause great harm.

According to standards set by the United States government, a person who works with ionizing radiation—such as an employee at a nuclear power plant or an X-ray technician—should get no more than five rems a year. People who are not radiation workers are normally exposed to much less radiation. Small amounts of radiation are usually expressed in millirems (a thousand millirems equals one rem).

People who work with radioactive materials wear devices that detect and record their exposure to ionizing radiation.

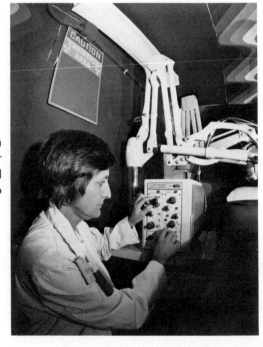

In a year's time, everyone on earth receives at least 30 millirems of radiation from cosmic rays. The atmosphere shields us from greater radiation doses, but its protection is reduced in high places, such as mountainous areas where the air is thinner than at sea level. And since cosmic radiation is deflected away from the equator by the earth's magnetism, it is most intense near the north and south poles.

As a result of these factors, people who live in the Rocky Mountains may get more than a hundred millirems of this radiation each year. People in jet aircraft, which commonly fly between 30,000 and 40,000 feet above sea level, receive more intense cosmic rays. A flight across the United States yields a dose of about two millirems, and a polar flight path exposes people to even more radiation. Crews of jet airliners receive as much radiation as many workers in nuclear power plants. A thousand hours of high-altitude flight annually gives them a thousand millirems or one rem of cosmic rays.

Cosmic radiation is much more intense in high-flying aircraft than it is at ground level.

For most people, however, the greatest source of natural radiation is their immediate surroundings on land. Ash from the 1980 eruption of Mount St. Helens in Washington contained the radioactive elements radon, radium, and thorium. Normally, radiation from the earth is mostly gamma rays emitted from radioactive elements in rocks, minerals, and soils. Like cosmic radiation, the levels of this radiation vary from place to place. Radiation "hot spots" exist in parts of France, Brazil, Egypt, and India. The highest levels of background radiation on earth are found in the Kerala region of India, an area of highly radioactive rocks and sands. Most residents receive 1,500 millirems of natural radiation a year. Some get twice this amount.

All over the earth, radiation reaches people directly from rocks and soils. It may also be emitted from water, and from bricks, cinderblocks, concrete, and other building materials made from rocks and minerals. People who live in brick houses receive more gamma rays than those who live in wooden houses.

Another source of radiation in our homes is radon gas. It diffuses out of rocks, soil, and building materials as a decay product of the element radium. (Geologists believe that a sudden increase in emission of radon from the earth may signal an impending earthquake.) Radon collects in basements and the

Every living thing contains some radioactive isotopes, including these which may be found in specific parts of the human body.

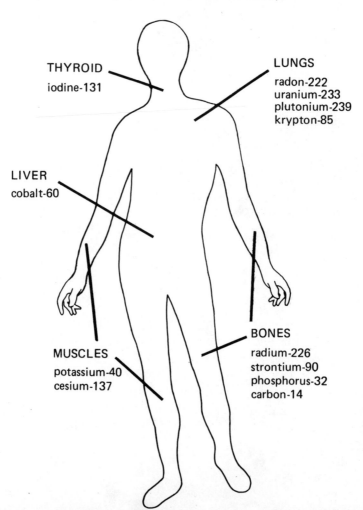

THYROID
iodine-131

LUNGS
radon-222
uranium-233
plutonium-239
krypton-85

LIVER
cobalt-60

BONES
radium-226
strontium-90
phosphorus-32
carbon-14

MUSCLES
potassium-40
cesium-137

ground floors of buildings, where the gas is usually much more concentrated than outdoors. In one Maine home, radon emitted from the water supply caused radiation levels to reach as high as those found in uranium mines.

As radon isotopes decay, they change to another unstable radioactive form, called radon daughters. These isotopes cling readily to bits of dust. The dust lodges in lungs when inhaled, and alpha radiation from the radon daughters can damage lung cells and cause cancer. There is growing concern about radon, as well as other air pollutants, that occurs in the air inside homes and other buildings (especially those that have been made more airtight to conserve energy).

Other kinds of radiation enter our bodies as we breathe, drink, and eat. Cereals and nuts are especially high in natural radiation. Fruits contain very little. But virtually all food contains some radioactive isotopes. The most common in our bodies are potassium-40, carbon-14, and tritium (hydrogen-3). Cigarette smokers take polonium-210, from tobacco plants, into their lungs. Everyone has some thorium and uranium inside his or her body. Not only do we receive some radiation from our bones and tissues, but our bodies give off ionizing radiation to our surroundings, including other people. Humans irradiate one another, but mostly they irradiate themselves, since nearly all of the radiation stays within us.

The radiation inside our bodies represents just 20 millirems— the smallest part of the total background radiation on earth. In all, people receive an average of about 100 millirems each of radiation a year. Most of this is unavoidable. Any ionizing radiation can be harmful, however, and even this small amount causes some deaths from cancer. How many, it is difficult to say. Because of the nature of cancer and of radiation, it is impossible to say one cancer was caused by cosmic rays, and another by radon daughters given off from the basement walls.

Some scientists estimate that natural background radiation in the United States may cause as many as 45,000 cancer deaths each year, but others believe this estimate is much too high. Helpful evidence may come from studies conducted in those areas that have the highest levels of background radiation.

A duplicate of Little Boy, the atomic bomb that destroyed much of Hiroshima, Japan, in 1945.

Among people studied in the Kerala region of India, for example, no unusual incidence of leukemia was found, even though this form of cancer is usually one of the first results of excessive exposure to radiation. Another study among Kerala residents showed a high incidence of a kind of mental retardation. A similar study in a Chinese region of high background radiation also found an excess of this condition. The trustworthiness of this research is in doubt, however. In fact, many studies conducted to determine the effects of radiation on populations have been criticized as inadequate. Some surveys consider too small a population to draw legitimate conclusions. And a cancer study that checks the health of people exposed to radiation but which lasts only ten years is useless, since many cancers require more than ten years to develop. Though some people say that

The effects of radioactivity from atomic bombs on Japanese people are still being studied.

there is no evidence that small amounts of radiation are harmful, it is often more accurate to say that there has been no adequate study. The evidence, whatever it is, has yet to be revealed.

There is no doubt about the harm caused by high doses of radiation. We have learned about this mainly from the Japanese victims of atomic bombs dropped during World War II. Many thousands died instantly, and many thousands more died after a few days of acute radiation sickness, as a result of exposure to gamma rays.

The first signs of radiation sickness are nausea and vomiting. The victim may feel better for a while, but in a few days other symptoms appear. They include fever, loss of hair, and breakdown of the nervous and circulatory systems. A heavy dose of ionizing radiation may destroy nerve cells, the cells that line the digestive tract, and the tissues that produce white blood cells. In such cases, chances of recovery are slim because the body's defenses against infection are lost.

Doses of 800 rads or more are always fatal. Half of the people exposed to 450 rads will die. Some die when they receive just 200 rads of radiation. At doses of 50 rads or less, there are no immediate outward signs of illness in humans.

Some animals are more resistant to radiation. Rabbits and mice can withstand about twice as much radiation as people. Half of a fruit fly population lives after exposure to 80,000 rads. And half of a cockroach population survives a dose of 100,000 rads.

Even though people suffer no immediate effects from exposure to 50 rads or less, the radiation can have long-term effects. When radiation penetrates deeply into the body, it may kill or damage cells, or parts of cells. Genes in sex cells may be harmed. In a sense, genes represent a set of directions that help determine the characteristics of the next generation. Changes in these genetic directions are called mutations, and ionizing radiation causes an increase in mutations. Exposing sex cells to radiation is like firing a bullet into a computer. There is no way to tell what change will result, or whether it will be harmful.

According to one study among children conceived by Japanese survivors of atomic explosions, there was a slight increase in birth defects or other signs of harmful mutations. Once again,

Survivors in Nagasaki and Hiroshima later suffered from an abnormal incidence of leukemia and other cancers.

scientists disagree about the adequacy of the research. However, many studies of mice and other small mammals, and of such insects as fruit flies, show that radiation does cause harmful mutations. These experiments reveal that even the smallest amount of radiation can cause mutations in sex cells. There is no absolutely safe dose of ionizing radiation.

Children are especially vulnerable to radiation, and they are most susceptible before birth, as developing embryos or fetuses. Early in its development an embryo is made up of relatively few, rapidly multiplying cells. Radiation damage to some of these embryonic cells can cause death or serious abnormalities. Even after two to four months of growth, a human fetus that is exposed to ionizing radiation may develop into a mentally retarded or physically deformed child.

Among the survivors of atomic explosions in Japan were some pregnant women. Some of their fetuses died just after their exposure to radiation, some at birth, and some lived only a short time. Most of the children who lived were mentally retarded, and as adults have been less able to resist disease than others who were not irradiated in the womb.

Besides causing mutations and harming embryos and fetuses, ionizing radiation can cause cancer. Actually, a radiation-damaged cell is more dangerous than a cell that is destroyed by radiation. A dead cell cannot reproduce itself. A damaged cell repairs itself, and can divide again and again. A cancerous growth may result from such an altered cell.

Cancer can develop in many parts of the body, and usually does so slowly. It may appear more than twenty years after exposure to radiation or to another cause of cancer. Usually the first to develop is leukemia, cancer of the blood. Within two years of the atomic blasts in Japan, an unusual incidence of leukemia was seen among the survivors. As the years have passed since World War II, the population of Japanese survivors has had an abnormal amount of cancer of the thyroid gland, salivary gland, breast, and colon. There is other evidence, among uranium miners for example, that ionizing radiation can cause cancer.

Fortunately, most people are not exposed to much radiation. Nevertheless, the most cautious health experts stress that there is no safe dose of ionizing radiation. We know that we will always live with some natural background radiation, but we must be more alert to other, human-made sources that have become common in this century.

X-rays 3

Soon after Wilhelm Roentgen discovered the radiation he called X-rays, its medical value was recognized and put to use. Before 1900, X-rays were used to locate bullets and shrapnel in wounded British soldiers. X-rays have since become a vital aid to doctors and dentists. During 1980, about 86 million people in the United States received dental X-rays, and 161 million received medical X-rays. This accounted for about 90 percent of the public's exposure to all human-made radiation.

A minor part of this exposure is X-rays that are emitted from color television sets, which are basically low-voltage X-ray devices. All television sets made since 1970 were designed to limit the X-ray emission to a half-millirem per hour. Human exposure is a small fraction of this if people stay several feet away from the television screen.

Many uses have been found for X-rays. They and other penetrating radiation are widely used in industry, to check the quality of metal welds, for example. At one time, shoe stores had machines that used X-rays to give customers a view of their feet inside shoes they tried on. Early research also showed that X-rays aimed at tumors killed these growths, so doctors believed that X-rays could cure cancer. Eventually this radiation was used for all sorts of major and minor ailments, even though it was not known to be effective in many cases. Millions of people received X-ray therapy for acne, ringworm, and other skin disorders. People with asthma and whooping cough were treated with X-rays. It became routine to irradiate people, including children, infants, and pregnant women.

Although scientists were concerned about X-rays causing genetic mutations, they did not suspect that ionizing radiation could cause cancer. Beginning in 1902, however, evidence of X-ray harm began to appear. Eventually some dentists developed skin cancer on their fingers—the same fingers they used to hold film in position in their patients' mouths as X-rays were taken. By doing this many times a year, they received much more radiation than any one patient. They did not know the X-rays penetrating their hands and bodies were dangerous. Deaths from cancer among dentists and X-ray technicians showed that it was.

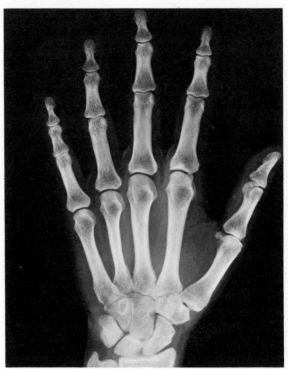

Each year more than 161 million people in the United States receive medical X-rays.

In 1944, after studying the obituaries in a medical journal over a span of years, a doctor reported that radiologists who worked regularly with X-ray machines were ten times more likely to die from leukemia than other physicians. Cancer was also found to occur more frequently than usual in people who had been treated with heavy doses of X-rays. For example, there was an increase in thyroid cancer among adults who, as children, had received X-ray treatment of ringworm on their scalps.

Most cancers develop slowly, so many years passed before the dangers of X-rays became clear. Since then, medical and health officials have tried to reduce the amount of human X-ray exposure and have had some success. Chest X-rays were once the routine way to detect tuberculosis; now skin tests are used. Much greater care is taken to avoid X-raying embryos or fetuses within pregnant women. Improved equipment, film, and shielding have also helped reduce the radiation dose of each exposure.

Despite these gains, many people are still exposed to unnecessary risk from X-rays. An estimated third of all diagnostic X-rays are not needed. Patients sometimes insist on having an X-ray when it is unnecessary. Doctors may order X-rays taken simply to protect themselves against malpractice suits brought by patients claiming that a medical problem was overlooked. Employers may insist that employees have annual chest X-rays, and such X-rays are also given to any patient admitted for any reason to certain hospitals. Many dentists still routinely X-ray patients at each each six-month checkup.

In 1979, the Food and Drug Administration found that one third of dental X-ray machines and almost half of breast X-ray machines emitted excessive radiation. In 1980, a Congressional committee reported that people were also exposed to excess radiation because many operators of X-ray machines were poorly trained.

Every time a dentist takes an X-ray of your teeth, the skin closest to the machine receives about 1,000 millirems of radiation. This is ten times the average amount of background radiation your whole body receives in a year. Usually several X-rays are taken, so a person may receive between 4,000 and 8,000 millirems in his mouth. This is doubled if the dentist takes X-rays twice a year, as some do.

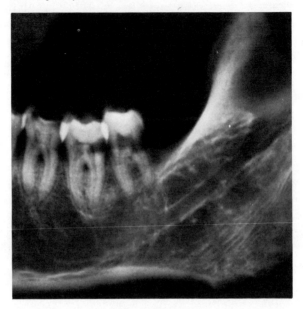

X-rays are vital in dental care, but faulty X-ray machines and overuse of X-rays expose patients to unnecessary risk.

This much radiation absorbed by a whole body is known to be harmful, but it is less dangerous when delivered to a small part of the body. Also, radiation given to a person's mouth is much less dangerous than that directed at the sex glands, breasts, eyes, or thyroid gland. Nevertheless, medical experts agree: the less radiation the better. The American Dental Association advises that X-rays should not be given routinely, but only when a dentist has no other way to get the information he or she needs. Young children with "baby teeth" should not be X-rayed. Many adults with healthy teeth can go several years without dental X-rays. For people who get cavities frequently, mouth X-rays once in two years should be sufficient.

Dentists should use a lead-rubber apron to protect patients. These aprons should be draped around a person's neck and lap to shield the thyroid gland, sex glands, and chest from scattered

X-rays. Dispersal of X-rays is greatly reduced if the dental X-ray machine emits radiation through a long, lead-lined cylinder, but many dentists still use a short, plastic, pointed cone that allows radiation to scatter. This makes it all the more important that pregnant women be shielded by a lead apron, or avoid exposure to X-rays entirely. (Fortunately, there are now devices that use reflections of sound waves to create visual images of the insides of bodies, so in many cases pregnant women no longer need to be X-rayed.)

A typical chest X-ray involves a front and a back view recorded on two pieces of film, and a total exposure of about 90 millirems. Health experts agree that the danger from a chest

Chest X-rays of normal lungs (left) and cancerous lungs (right).

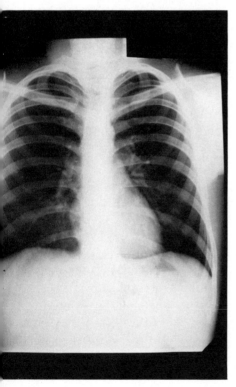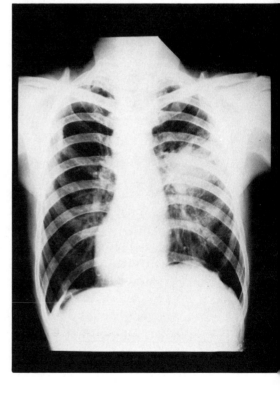

X-ray is low, but they advocate having as few as possible. In 1980, the American Cancer Society revised its cancer detection tests, stating that annual chest X-rays might do more harm than good, especially among young people.

A few years earlier the cancer society and the National Cancer Institute sponsored a national program to detect breast cancer. Several hundred thousand women were given breast X-rays (mammographs). The program's aim was to detect breast cancer at its early, treatable stages. The program is credited with saving thousands of lives, but it also may have caused harm.

The human breast is quite sensitive to radiation. In 1977, the National Cancer Institute concluded that repeated mammographs of women might be dangerous, because X-rays might cause more cancer than they detect. The institute ended routine breast X-rays of women under the age of 50, except for individuals who are suspected to be more likely than others to develop cancer. In 1982, however, research results showed that improved kinds of mammographs of younger women were able to detect many cancers that were missed by physical examinations. Furthermore, mammography discovered cancers in early stages of development, when most of them can be cured. If supported by other research, these findings might influence the National Cancer Institute to change its guidelines for detecting breast cancer.

Although there is growing concern about the misuse of X-rays, no one doubts that they are one of the most important tools in medicine. X-ray photos allow a peek into the body without surgery. Besides producing the usual photos, X-rays are used in the process called fluoroscopy, which provides an interior view of the body as it "operates"—digesting, breathing, circulating blood, and so on. A fluoroscope takes a series of X-ray photos and projects them on a screen as a moving picture, which can be filmed for later study. Although the newest fluoroscopes use less radiation than before, the process exposes people to much more radiation than a standard chest X-ray. The potential danger is greater, and fluoroscopy should be used sparingly, and only in certain medical situations. Those shoe-fit viewing machines mentioned earlier were a kind of fluoroscope. Their use was halted because there is nothing routine or casual about long X-ray exposure.

One of the most remarkable uses of X-rays was developed in the late 1960's. It is called the CAT scanner. The word CAT stands for *c*omputerized *a*xial *t*omography. As a CAT scanner rotates around a person's body or head, thin beams of X-rays enter the person and the different amounts of radiation absorbed within are measured by detectors. This information is processed by a computer, which then produces a television picture that is a thin cross section of the part being scanned. Usually a slice about a centimeter across is seen in sharp focus. Many of these cross sections from the computer's memory can be combined to form a complete three-dimensional picture of an organ.

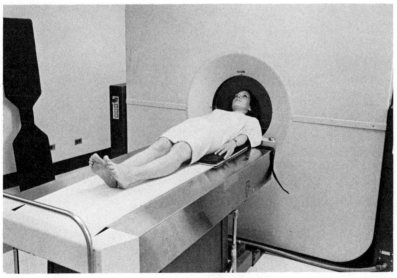

CAT scans have been especially valuable in the study and treatment of the brain.

The image or "scan" taken by this machine is much more finely detailed than an ordinary X-ray photo. CAT scans distinguish overlapping objects and detect slight differences in the density of tissues and organs. They are especially useful in picturing the brain. CAT machines specifically designed to

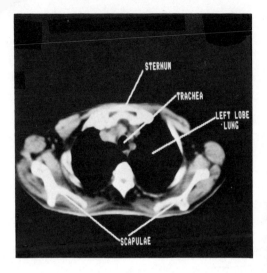

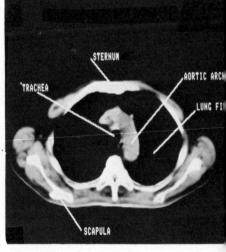

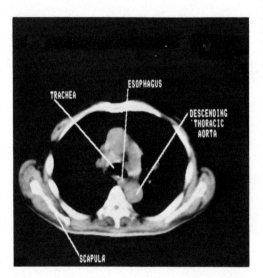

These three CAT scans (above) show cross-section views of a man's chest, including ribs and backbone. The scans on the facing page show several cross sections of a human brain.

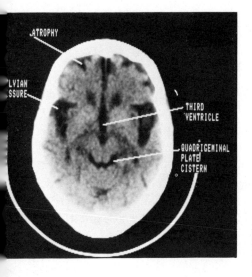

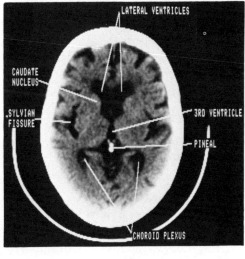

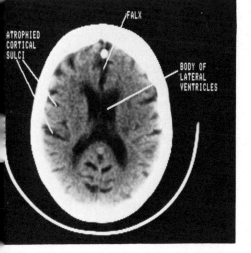

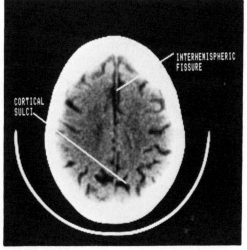

scan the head have become vital in the study and treatment of brain diseases and injuries.

Brain scans have replaced some dangerous and painful methods formerly used by doctors. They have saved lives. In one case, a girl struck by a car was brought to a hospital with a head injury. From her behavior, doctors thought that she was suffering from a hemorrhage, with blood flowing from injured veins and pressing against her brain. Ordinarily this is treated by drilling several holes in the skull to release the blood and relieve the pressure. But a CAT scan showed that there was no hemorrhage. The brain itself was greatly swollen. The girl's brain might have been severely damaged if holes had been drilled in her skull. Doctors were able to treat her with drugs to reduce the swelling and she recovered quickly.

Whole-body CAT scanners are useful in detecting cancers, including those for which there is no treatment. This spares people needless surgery. But there is growing concern about the overuse of these CAT scanners. They are like a new toy or gadget and have been called the "Cadillacs of medical technology." Hospitals, doctors, and patients all succumb to the appeal and status of using them. CAT scanners are sometimes used when cheaper and equally effective methods would suffice, and use of the scanners gives patients unneeded radiation.

A whole-body CAT scanner costs nearly a million dollars. Some medical authorities believe that the purchase of several hundred of these devices nationally has been a terrible waste of the limited funds that are available for health care. Others defend the purchase of CAT scanners, especially the most up-to-date models that are far advanced over early versions. They take a complete body scan in one second, rather than about two minutes. This produces clearer pictures, widens the possibilities of medical finds, and also reduces X-ray exposure.

Some physicians predict that CAT scanners may soon be supplanted by another device for peeking into bodies and heads. The technique is called NMR, or *n*uclear *m*agnetic *r*esonance tomography. It involves placing an object in a magnetic field, exciting its atoms with radio waves, and measuring the intensity of the waves that are emitted. The images that result are more detailed than those from CAT scanners. Clinical tests on humans began in 1980. NMR scanners are likely to be cheaper than CAT scanners to install and operate. They may be safer too, since they use no X-rays.

Sometimes a person has little choice but to be exposed to strong doses of X-rays. They are a major weapon against cancerous growths. Daily short exposures over a period of weeks or months are most effective. Radiologists must aim beams of X-rays precisely in order to kill cancer cells with a minimum of risk to nearby healthy cells. Fortunately, cancer cells are often more vulnerable to ionizing radiation than normal cells.

Such X-ray therapy has saved many lives, and there is no doubt that X-rays are needed to help detect and cure illness. The challenge is to stop their unnecessary use.

Radioactivity 4

The word radiation stirs up feelings of fear in many people—fear of something invisible and deadly. These feelings can be traced to past explosions of atomic bombs, and to the ever-present threat of nuclear war.

People tend to focus on the destruction and death that would be caused by atomic bombs or nuclear power accidents. However, there are many everyday uses of radioactive substances, such as nuclear power, that add low levels of radiation to our lives.

All nuclear power plants now in operation produce power through a process called nuclear fission—the splitting apart of the nuclei of atoms. When this happens to very heavy nuclei, such as those of uranium atoms, great amounts of heat energy are released. The heat is used to boil water, and steam from it is then used to generate electricity. In 1981, nuclear power provided about 12 percent of the electricity used in the United States.

Uranium-235 is the basic fuel of nuclear power plants. When neutrons bombard uranium-235 atoms causing fission, the unstable uranium atoms change. They decay, releasing neutrons,

and are converted to such lighter atoms as strontium and iodine.
The neutrons they emit cause the fission of other uranium-235
atoms, releasing more neutrons that, in turn, strike still more
uranium atoms. This process is called a chain reaction. Under
control, it produces a steady supply of heat energy, though
occasionally the plant must be shut down and refueled with
uranium.

Nuclear reactors are enclosed in typical dome-shaped concrete structures
at Indian Point, on the Hudson River north of New York City.

Fission takes place in a reactor chamber made of steel. Its
walls are at least eight inches thick. The reactor sits within a
concrete building—a further defense to keep much radiation
from escaping during routine operation, though probably not in
the event of a major accident.

Struck by a neutron, a uranium-235 atom splits and gives off energy and
neutrons, which then cause other atoms to fission.

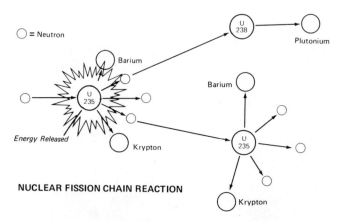

NUCLEAR FISSION CHAIN REACTION

One possible accident, called a meltdown, would occur if cooling water was lost, allowing the fuel core to heat rapidly, melt, and burn through the floor or wall, releasing radiation to the soil or air. Though a reactor cannot explode like a bomb, it contains much more radioactive material than the atomic weapons that were used on Japan. Radioactive debris from a reactor accident would include uranium, plutonium, krypton, and xenon. According to government studies, a reactor meltdown accident might kill thousands of people and damage at least $14 billion in property.

As of 1982, no such accident had occurred anywhere in the world. Nuclear proponents believed that extraordinary safety measures at nuclear plants would maintain that record. Others believed that a major disaster at a reactor was almost inevitable, largely because nuclear power plants are complex and are designed, built, and operated by humans, who make mistakes.

In normal operation, the inside surface of a reactor chamber is bombarded with neutrons and other radiation. After years of use the steel becomes brittle and weakens. This worried some engineers on the staff of the Nuclear Regulatory Commission, but little attention was paid to their concern. By 1981 about 20 of 72 reactors in the United States were old enough to have weakened chamber walls. Only then did the top officials of the Nuclear Regulatory Commission become alarmed about the possibility that a reactor chamber might crack. This might allow cooling water to flow out, and quickly lead to a meltdown, with radiation escaping through the crack.

A belated effort by the Commission to deal with this problem did not reassure the public. Confidence in the safety of nuclear power had already been undermined by the 1979 reactor accident at Three Mile Island, near Harrisburg, Pennsylvania. Besides losing public support, the nuclear industry had other troubles. The cost of new plants rose rapidly, the growth in demand for electricity dropped, and utilities stopped building some plants and canceled many reactor orders. Growth of nuclear power in the United States slowed. However, dozens of plants were in operation, using uranium fuel and producing radioactive wastes.

The nuclear fuel cycle, from mining to waste storage, exposes both workers and the public to some ionizing radiation. Uranium miners inhale radon gas while working. Many of those who mined during the 1940's and 1950's died of lung cancer and other lung diseases. The U.S. Labor Department now requires ventilators and other devices to reduce the amount of radiation. Its standards were made more strict in 1977, as studies showed that uranium miners still had a high incidence of lung cancer. The miners' union claims that the standards are still not tough enough and are not well-enforced.

Exposed to radioactive radon as they work, many uranium miners have died of lung cancer.

Workers are also exposed to radiation as uranium is milled, enriched, transported, used as fuel, and stored. During these operations, some of the public may be exposed to radioactivity as well. For decades, the waste ore from uranium processing—called tailings—was simply left in piles on the land. Tailings resemble fine sand. In some areas they were used as fill before construction, or in concrete used for the foundations of thousands of homes and other buildings. People in these buildings were exposed to high levels of radiation, especially from radon. Some in Colorado received radiation equal to having more than 550 chest X-rays in a year. Since the problem was discovered, many buildings have been rebuilt at government expense.

River water and underground water supplies have also been contaminated by radiation from tailings. (Wastes from phosphate mining also release radon and are a possible health risk to people in parts of Florida, Idaho, and Montana.) To reduce the threat of radon from uranium tailings, in 1978 the federal government began the long, expensive task of covering and, in some cases, moving and burying 25 million tons of tailings from abandoned uranium mills. Meanwhile, active mills have produced new piles of tailings, totaling 172 million tons—an even larger and more costly disposal problem.

People who work with uranium throughout its fuel cycle are supposed to receive no more than five rems of radiation annually. On the average they receive one rem or less on the job. Protective clothing and shielding devices help reduce exposure. The need to protect workers from excess radiation creates problems, for example, when many skilled welders must be hired to make repairs so that none receive too much radiation. For some unskilled jobs, the nuclear industry hires people temporarily to work in places where they receive high levels of radiation. Then they are laid off until enough time passes so they are again eligible for more radiation exposure. Such

To minimize exposure to radiation, workers use mechanical hands which mimic their hand movements and handle dangerous isotopes within a sealed enclosure.

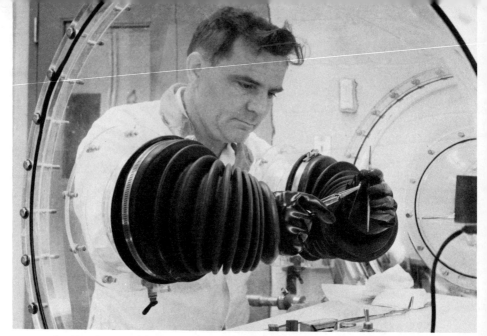

A glove box enables a person to handle radioactive isotopes directly inside an enclosure while he or she remains outside.

workers are called sponges or jumpers. About 30,000 are employed each year. Their use allows more highly skilled employees to work longer hours. It remains to be seen whether sponges are harmed by their exposure to radioactivity.

Not just uranium fuel but all sorts of other radioactive substances used in medicine and industry must be moved from one place to another. Special containers and other precautions are supposed to guarantee safety, but transportation of radioactive materials has been barred from some areas. So far there has been little transport of nuclear wastes away from power plants. Most of the spent fuel from reactors is stored in deep pools of water at power plant sites. The water must be constantly cooled, filtered, and recirculated. Though nuclear reactors have operated commercially since 1958, the question of what to do with their wastes has not been answered. Wastes from the production of

The diagram on the next page shows steps in radioactive decay, as unstable isotopes with different half-lives eventually reach a stable form.

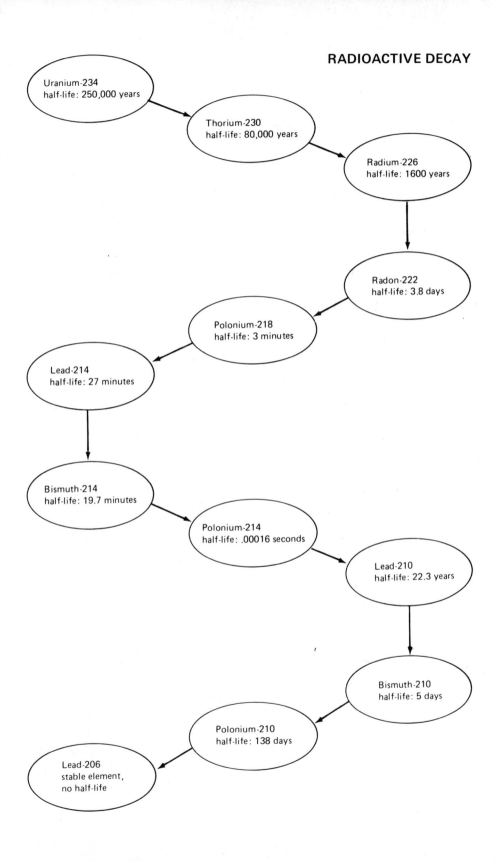

RADIOACTIVE DECAY

Uranium-234
half-life: 250,000 years

Thorium-230
half-life: 80,000 years

Radium-226
half-life: 1600 years

Radon-222
half-life: 3.8 days

Polonium-218
half-life: 3 minutes

Lead-214
half-life: 27 minutes

Bismuth-214
half-life: 19.7 minutes

Polonium-214
half-life: .00016 seconds

Lead-210
half-life: 22.3 years

Bismuth-210
half-life: 5 days

Polonium-210
half-life: 138 days

Lead-206
stable element,
no half-life

nuclear weapons and other uses of radioactive elements are also a problem. This concerns many people as much as the possibility of a reactor accident.

Spent fuel from a reactor can be kept in special pools or aboveground concrete structures for decades. During this time some radioactive elements become harmless as they decay. The rate of decay is called an element's half-life. It is the time needed for half of the original amount of an element to decay to other atoms. For example, iodine-131, which is present in the spent reactor fuel, has a half-life of eight days. After eight days a pound of iodine-131 would have become a half pound of iodine-131 and a half pound of other elements. After another eight days a quarter pound of iodine-131 would remain. Only a tiny fraction would be left after 20 half-lives. At this point a radioactive isotope like iodine-131 can be considered harmless.

Other unstable isotopes in nuclear wastes have much longer half-lives. Strontium-90 decays by emitting beta particles and has a half-life of 30 years. Plutonium-239 decays by emitting alpha particles and has a half-life of 24,000 years. A quantity of this substance would not be harmless until at least a quarter-million years had passed. For some reactor wastes probably the only possible safe storage place is deep underground, in rock or salt formations that are likely to remain undisturbed long into the future. Some scientists have confidence in this plan. Others are skeptical and worry that radioactive substances might enter ground water and reach the surface eventually, still capable of harming life.

Although there seem to be good reasons to be concerned about nuclear wastes and about mishaps at reactors, the normal operations of the nuclear fuel cycle add very little radiation to the lives of most of the public. Government regulations allow very low levels of radiation to leave nuclear power plants in cooling water and in the air. Utilities are required to limit exposure outside the boundary fence of a power plant to just a few millirems a year. Many people get this much radiation simply by being inside brick, stone, or concrete buildings for a few weeks. Also, a coal-fired power plant emits into the air about the same amount of radiation as a nuclear plant, since coal contains small amounts of uranium and thorium. This fact is often quoted by promoters of nuclear power. A more thorough comparison reveals that the nuclear fuel cycle brings from 35 to 81 times more radioactive material to the earth's surface than the coal fuel cycle. Also, overall comparison of the health effects of coal and nuclear plants must take into account that only nuclear plants have the potential of a catastrophic accident.

In addition to receiving one or two millirems of radiation from the nuclear fuel cycle, each person in the United States also gets some radiation from tests of nuclear weapons. This may seem odd, since most aboveground testing of nuclear bombs ceased in the mid-1960's. Most of the radioactive debris from these explosions fell to earth soon afterward, but some of the particles rose high into the atmosphere and are still drifting down. In 1980, everyone in the northern hemisphere received an estimated four and a half millirems of radiation from bomb fallout. Some of this fallout is inhaled or swallowed. Virtually everyone contains some strontium-90 and plutonium-239 that came from a nuclear explosion.

Between 1946 and 1964, the United States exploded 183 nuclear weapons aboveground. Bomb tests in the western United States began in 1951. About 103,000 soldiers and other military personnel were exposed to radiation from blasts at close range. In parts of Nevada, Utah, and Arizona, residents in the path of fallout also received large doses of radiation. At that time, most scientists believed that people could safely absorb a dose of 25 rems. Troops and the public were assured that there was no danger.

Army troops watch a nuclear weapon explode at Yucca Flats, Nevada, in 1951.

Sheep provided the first sign that scientists had underestimated the hazard. In 1953, after several bomb tests, more than 4,000 sheep died in Utah and Nevada. Ranchers suspected that radiation caused the deaths, but lost a suit for damages brought against the government. In 1982, however, a judge ordered a new trial, because documents showed that the government had withheld evidence that radiation had harmed the sheep.

Troops were placed within a few miles of the blasts. Shortly after some tests they marched to ground zero—the actual explosion site. Many of the troops wore special film badges that were supposed to record their exposure to radiation. The blasts emitted mostly neutron, alpha, and beta particles. Desert dust stirred up by the explosions undoubtedly was contaminated by alpha particles, and some of it was inhaled by those who witnessed the tests.

It appears that troops who were at the tests suffered from a high rate of radiation-caused illness and death. This is being investigated, but the full story may never be known because of incomplete records of who was present and how much radiation they received. In 1982 a former Army medic revealed that he had been ordered to keep two sets of records at four Nevada atomic tests. One gave false, low film-badge readings from troops exposed to radiation at or near ground zero. The other gave the true and much higher radiation doses the men actually received. According to the medic, he had been warned that he could be charged with treason if he told about the false radiation data.

High levels of radiation were recorded in small communities located many miles from the test. Citizens in a Utah town 145 miles from the test site received a dose of six rems in one day following a 1953 explosion. In 1962, a study by the Public Health Service found an increase in leukemia deaths in Utah. Eventually, leukemia deaths among children in southern Utah were found to be two and a half times the normal rate. It was 1980, however, before an interagency panel of the federal government officially acknowledged that the bomb tests had caused death and disease among people who lived downwind from the blasts.

Unless there is more aboveground bomb-testing or actual nuclear war, the amount of fallout will continue to decline slowly. Other sources of human-made radiation exposure may be reduced too. Less radium is used on the dials of watches and clocks than before. Particles emitted by radium make the phosphorescent paint glow in the dark. Some of the early evidence of the risks of radiation came from workers who put paint containing radium on watch dials. They commonly put their paint brushes to their lips to make a fine point. The radium they ingested eventually gave many of them bone cancer.

Photographed with boxes of clock faces at their sides, these women were ready for another day of painting with radium, unaware that it would give many of them cancer.

Radium has been replaced by tritium. Low-energy beta particles from tritium do not pass easily through glass or plastic watch crystals. Radium is also used in smoke detectors, although the most commonly used isotope is americium-241. It emits alpha particles, which are totally spent within a few inches of their source. Americium-241, however, has a half-life of 433 years, and the expected useful life of the 40 million smoke detectors in the United States is just ten years. Thus, after smoke detectors are thrown away, radiation from americium-241 will still be somewhere on the earth's surface. There is growing worry about other long-lived radioactive materials used in a variety of electronic devices and glow-in-the-dark products. Whether incinerated or buried in a landfill, most of the radioactivity from these objects will remain in our lives for several centuries.

Radioactive substances have many beneficial uses in medicine and industry. They may be swallowed, injected, or implanted as part of cancer therapy. Plutonium-238 is a power source in cardiac pacemakers, which are surgically placed under the skin of people who have irregular heart beats. The pacemaker generates electrical impulses that cause heart muscles to work at a normal rhythm. The radioactive power source needs to be replaced only once in about ten years—a vast improvement over batteries. The pacemaker also gives its wearer about 5,000 millirems of radiation a year, and exposes family members and others to much smaller amounts. In the opinion of most physicians, the benefits of radioactive heart pacemakers seem to outweigh the risks.

Plutonium-238 is the common power source of cardiac pacemakers, which help regulate heartbeats.

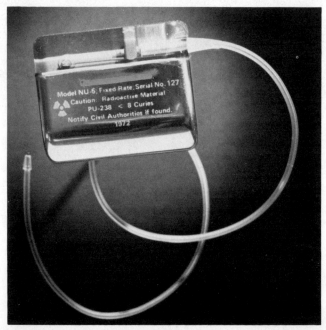

Radioactive substances can be used to diagnose and treat diseases. The substance may be swallowed in liquid form—a "radioactive cocktail"—or injected into the blood stream. It serves as a tracer, as radiation detectors outside the body enable doctors to follow the movements of the substance and check the inner workings of the body.

Certain elements become concentrated in particular parts of the body, and this is useful both in diagnosing and treating diseases. Iodine, for example, settles in the thyroid gland. Doctors use radioactive iodine-131 as a tracer and measure the amount in the thyroid gland over a period of time to see how well the gland functions. An overactive thyroid can also be treated effectively with iodine-131, though there is an increased risk that cancer will be caused by particles given off as it decays.

After a radioactive isotope is injected or swallowed, its course through the body can be traced by radioactive detectors.

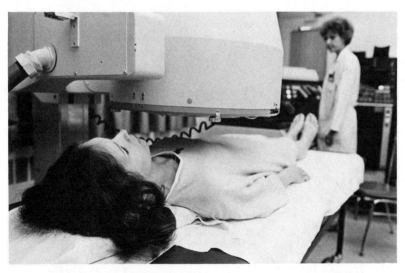

Each year at least 700,000 people receive iodine-131 to diagnose or treat thyroid disorders. Some patients are given more radiation than necessary. They irradiate people around them, and members of their families are more likely than others to get thyroid cancer. According to two physicians at Harvard University, some patients emit so much radiation that—had they been packages—government regulations would cause airlines to refuse them space as air cargo. As passengers, however, they can sit beside other people. The physicians said that the risk to other people is low, but stressed that medical radiation exposure is greater than it has to be.

Radioactive tracers are used in studies of both plants and animals. They enable biologists to "tag" small creatures, such as spiders, so that they can be located again with Geiger counters or other devices that detect and measure radioactivity. By tagging plants with phosphorous-32, then later detecting radioactivity among the small animals that fed on the plants, biologists have gained a better understanding of the flow of food energy in nature. Tracers are also used in industry to help measure flow rates and check for leaks in piping systems, or to check the thoroughness of mixing in oil refining tanks.

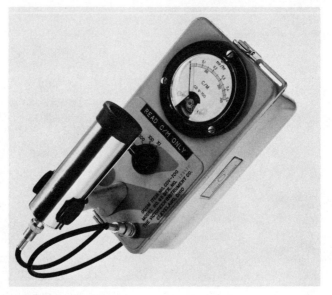

Portable Geiger counters are used to detect and measure levels of radioactivity.

In the early 1980's there was renewed interest in the use of radiation to preserve food. The process involves passing food in any form through a shielded chamber where it is briefly exposed to gamma or X-rays. The food does not become radioactive, but the radiation kills bacteria, retarding spoilage. Irradiation also slows the ripening of fruit and the sprouting of potatoes and onions. It would increase the safe storage time of foods in shipping, in stores, and in homes. The Food and Drug Administration was expected to approve low doses of radiation for this purpose, although some scientists warned that irradiation can cause chemical changes in foods, and the effects of these changes should be investigated first.

Leaves marked "control" were grown normally, while the others received 150 or more rems of gamma radiation over a two-month period.

If safe, food irradiation can save huge amounts of food from going to waste—another benefit to humans from radioactivity. But its use would also mean that more radioactive substances are being mined, refined, transported, and handled, and more wastes and radiation-tainted equipment must be buried or otherwise kept from contact with people. Even more than X-rays, the gamma rays and particles from radioactive elements are a mixed blessing.

Low-level Risks 5

Anyone who adds up the human-made ionizing radiation in his or her life usually gets a total well below 170 millirems a year. This is the recommended limit for public exposure set by the National Academy of Sciences in 1957. People who receive radiation therapy, or who live near uranium tailings are exposed to greater radioactivity. Nevertheless, their total exposure is usually less than five rems each—the limit set for people who actually work with radioactive substances.

Are these exposure levels really safe? This question has been asked a lot in recent years. The original limits set by the science academy were based mostly on studies of Japanese survivors of atomic explosions and also of people who received X-ray therapy. In other words, they were based on people who had experienced one or a few exposures to high doses of radio-activity. The government's standard is applied to people who experience radiation differently—receiving low doses over a long period.

Some scientists believe that the risks of low-level radiation have been underestimated. Their belief is supported by research findings, though some of the results are disputed. One investigation found higher than usual rates of certain cancers among former employees of the Hanford Atomic Energy Reservation, a plant in the state of Washington that produces plutonium for nuclear weapons. The study's statistical methods were criticized, and it was suggested that chemicals at Hanford could have caused an increase in cancer. Another analysis of the Hanford research found no evidence of a chemical cause, and concluded that radiation was the only rational explanation of the cancers. A new investigation is under way.

Studies of mice and other small mammals show that low levels of ionizing radiation can cause harmful mutations.

In New England, one scientist believed he had discovered a high incidence of cancers, particularly leukemia, among shipyard workers who had repaired and refueled nuclear submarines. When he repeated the study with more complete data supplied by the Navy, his earlier findings were thrown into doubt. In Scotland, however, nuclear shipyard workers were found to have abnormalities in the genetic material of their cells. Similar cell damage was found among workers at a nuclear weapons plant in Colorado. In both places, workers had been exposed to less than five rems of radiation a year, the limit that is supposedly safe.

Nuclear shipyard workers may suffer ill effects from exposure to low levels of radioactivity in their workplace.

In the opinion of many scientists, most of this new evidence was flawed or incomplete, and did not make much of a case. Others urged that the risk estimates on radiation exposure be reexamined. In 1977, a committee of the National Academy of Sciences began a two-year study of all available evidence. The Committee on the Biological Effects of Ionizing Radiation (called the BEIR Committee) concluded in 1979 that the risks of low-level radiation are very small, but are potentially greater than believed before. The report estimated that one-half to one percent of the nation's population—up to one million people— would develop cancer from human-made sources of radiation sometime during their lives. A minority of the committee members disagreed and called the report "alarmist." One committee member said that "the public is incredibly over-concerned with radiation to the point of superstition."

Even as the BEIR Committee was coming to its conflicting

conclusions, new studies were being conducted. Scientists at two government research laboratories revised the estimated radiation experienced by the Japanese in the 1945 atomic bomb explosions. They concluded that there had been much less neutron radiation than previously thought, and lower gamma ray doses at the city of Nagasaki. This raised doubts about *all* earlier calculations of the effects of radioactivity on humans.

In light of the new findings, the individual radiation dose of each Japanese survivor would have to be refigured. If the new picture of bomb radiation was correct, this meant there was no good evidence for judging the effects of neutrons on people. It also suggested that gamma rays are more dangerous than assumed before. And this possibility seemed to be supported by the most up-to-date tally of increased cancer deaths among the Japanese survivors.

If low levels of ionizing radiation are more harmful than previously thought, their effects—genetic damage and cancers—will probably appear first among people who work with radioactive substances. In all, about a quarter-million people work with radiation in medicine and in scientific research. Many thousands more face radiation on the job in manufacturing and in military research. About 40,000 people, including so-called sponges, work in the nuclear fuel cycle. (Their overall exposure to radioactivity rose sharply in the early 1980's as a result of chronic maintenance problems at reactors.)

Although low-level radiation health risks to the public remain a matter of scientific controversy, some radiation workers may be in real danger. Special attention should be focused on women workers, since they seem to face a greater risk than men of developing radiation-induced cancer. Better programs of medical checkups and better records of radiation exposure will increase understanding of the risks—a vital first step toward reducing them. However, until there is greater agreement among scientists about the dangers of low-level radiation, there will be no change in the present exposure limits set for radioactivity.

Concern is becoming greater about other kinds of radiation, mentioned in the first chapter, that lie beyond infrared radiation—microwaves, radar, television and radio broadcasting, and extremely low frequency wavelengths. All of this radiation in nonionizing. It is not energetic enough to create ions from atoms and was long thought to be harmless. Now there is growing doubt about the safety of some wavelengths.

There is no question that high-intensity microwaves can damage and kill tissue. In a microwave oven, food molecules are excited as the waves of energy penetrate the food. This causes rapid movement of the molecules, which generates heat, rapid heating, and cooking. The ovens have safety features to minimize wave scattering while they're in use. They are designed to shut off automatically when their doors are opened. The health risk from the two million microwave ovens used in the United States seems to be slight, but ovens are only one use of microwaves.

They are emitted from television and radio broadcasting antennas, radar towers, and industrial machines that are used to seal plywood and plastics. People who work with such equipment are exposed to much more microwave radiation than the general public, though public exposure grows with the increase in products that use microwaves. In addition to ovens these include garage door openers, CB radios, burglar alarms, and anti-theft devices in retail stores.

In 1966, a safety standard for microwave and radar exposure was established. It was based on the idea that the only danger from microwaves was their heating effect. The safe limit was set at ten milliwatts per square centimeter of human skin. This is about one tenth the amount of microwave power needed to cause a heating effect, so it seemed to provide a wide margin of safety.

Some workers are exposed to microwaves beyond this standard. Between 40,000 and 80,000 people work with microwave heat sealers. In 1980, two hundred of these machines were checked and 60 percent were found to exceed the ten-milliwatt limit. Many workers receive somewhat less exposure but complain of such symptoms as fatigue and headaches.   In 1981, an Army pathologist reported evidence of a link between chronic exposure to microwaves and a rare blood disease.   He found a high incidence of the disease among radar operators.

Some military radar operators have won compensation from the Veterans Administration after developing cataracts on their eyes. And in 1974, the widow of a telephone technician won compensation from the New York Telephone Company for his microwave-induced death. Samuel Yannon had tuned television signals that were broadcast from the Empire State Building in New York City. After several years of this work he had troubled vision and hearing. He developed cataracts and eventually experienced a premature, abnormal aging and death.

Some evidence suggests that radar workers may be harmed by their exposure to microwaves.

Scientists in the Soviet Union and in eastern European countries have claimed for two decades that low microwave doses harm people. Their reported effects include headaches, decreased memory, irregular heart beats, genetic defects, and decreased fertility. The Soviet microwave safety limit is .01

milliwatt per square centimeter—a thousand times lower than the limit in the United States. In this nation there has been little research involving the long-term exposure to low-level microwaves. Many American scientists are skeptical about the quality and the validity of the Soviet research. They contend that the microwave doses to which most Americans are exposed are still far too low to cause harm.

There is growing concern, however, about the safety of the higher microwave doses that workers receive, and about the overall increase in microwave-emitting products. Too little is known, and more research is under way or planned. The question of how much microwave radiation a person can safely absorb may not be answered for a long time.

Radiation damage has been blamed on another electronic device, the video display terminal (VDT), which is used to display computer data in banks, offices, and businesses. These devices are used by nearly ten million workers in the United States. Workers who spend their days in front of VDTs complain of blurred vision, eye strain, headaches, and sometimes facial rashes. Some operators have blamed VDTs for cataracts or for genetic damage that led to birth defects in their offspring.

VDTs work much like television sets. They give off X-rays and microwaves. Investigations by government health agencies in Canada and the United States have found, however, that extremely low levels of radiation are emitted. The results of a Norwegian study suggested that an electrostatic field produced by VDTs was the cause of skin rashes. Headaches and vision problems seem to be caused by glare, too-bright room lights, and stress as workers move their eyes from papers to keyboards to screens up to 33,000 times a day. To blame VDTs for radiation damage, most scientists believe, will only divert attention from the real causes and slow the search for ways to reduce their effects on workers.

There are more important hazards already known, from X-rays, gamma rays, alpha rays, and other kinds of radiation. As soon as possible we need to know more about how living things are affected by these invisible waves and particles. And while we seek this knowledge, we must find ways to reduce the harmful radiation in our lives.

Glossary

alpha rays—charged particles, made up of two protons and two neutrons, that are emitted from the nucleus of a radioactive atom.

atom—the smallest unit of an element, consisting of a central nucleus surrounded by orbiting electrons.

beta rays—high-energy electrons emitted from radioactive atoms.

cancer—a disorder in which cells grow wildly, producing colonies called malignant neoplasms. These growths are made up of cells unlike those nearby and tend to spread through the body. Cancer is the second leading cause of death in the United States.

CAT scanner—a device which directs X-rays from many angles at an object (such as a person's head), detects the varying amounts of radiation absorbed, and organizes the X-ray images into a television picture of the object. The procedure is called computerized axial tomography.

cosmic rays—particles with great penetrating power that originate in stars and interact with atoms in the atmosphere to produce electrons, gamma rays, and other radiation.

electromagnetic field—the interaction of electric and magnetic forces in a given space produces an effect called an electromagnetic field.

electron—a negatively-charged particle of an atom which orbits its nucleus and is much lighter than a proton or neutron.

embryo—in humans, the unborn young from the time of conception to the age of two months.

fallout—radioactive fission products created by nuclear explosions, which fall from the atmosphere to the earth's surface.

fetus—in humans, the unborn young from the age of two months to birth.

fission—the process by which an atomic nucleus splits and produces heat energy and radioactive particles.

flouroscopy—the process that uses a continuous stream of X-rays to provide images of internal structures at work, either in living things or mechanical devices.

gamma rays—high-energy radiation of great penetrating power, emitted by nuclei of some radioactive elements.

Geiger counter—an instrument used to detect and measure radioactivity.

genes—protein molecules within sex cells that transmit traits or characteristics from parents to offspring.

half-life—the period of time in which half the nuclei in an amount of radioactive material undergo decay to another nuclear form. Some radioactive substances have half-lives of seconds; others have half-lives of thousands of years.

infrared radiation—nonionizing radiation having wavelengths longer than those of visible light.

ion—an atom or group of atoms carrying a positive or negative charge of electricity, as a result of losing or gaining electrons.

ionizing radiation—a type of radiation that is powerful enough to cause electrons to be emitted from atoms or to be added to them, thus producing ions with either a positive or negative charge.

isotope—an atom which has the same number of protons in its nucleus as other varieties of an element but which has a different number of neutrons. (Also called a radionuclide or nuclide.)

latent period—the span of time between exposure to a disease-causing agent and the development of disease to a stage where it can be detected.

leukemia—cancer of the blood. A disease of the tissues which produce white blood cells, causing an excess of abnormal cells in the blood.

mammograph—an X-ray image of a breast.

microwaves—nonionizing radiation having wavelengths between infrared and shortwave radio waves.

millirem—one thousandth of a rem, a unit that is a measure of dose to living tissue by ionizing radiation.

mutation—a change in the genetic material of a cell, which may result in offspring that are somewhat different from the parent.

neutron—an uncharged particle of an atomic nucleus. Neutrons are emitted at high speed during fission and can be absorbed by other nuclei.

NMR tomography—a process somewhat similar to CAT scanning, except that the more detailed images are a result of exposing an object to radio waves in a strong magnetic field. NMR stands for *n*uclear *m*agnetic *r*esonance.

proton—a positively charged particle which makes up part of the nucleus of an atom.

rad—a unit of ionizing radiation that is actually absorbed by living tissues. Rad stands for *r*adiation *a*bsorbed *d*ose.

radar—a method of detecting distant objects and determining their position, speed, and other characteristics by use of high-frequency (short-wavelength) radio waves reflected from the object. Radar stands for *ra*dio *d*etection *a*nd *r*anging.

radioactivity—behavior of a substance in which nuclei are undergoing change and emitting particles. This occurs naturally in about 50 elements and also can be produced artificially.

radiology—the science dealing with the use of ionizing radiation for diagnosing or treating disease.

rem—the unit of ionizing radiation that has the same biological effects as one rad of X-rays. It stands for *r*oentgen *e*quivalent *m*an.

tailings—gray, sandlike material left over from uranium ore processing. Tailings contain such radioactive elements as uranium and radium, and radon gas.

thyroid gland—a gland located in the neck of humans and all other animals with backbones. It produces the hormone thyroxin, which regulates many of the basic chemical processes of the body.

ultraviolet—nonionizing radiation having wavelengths between visible violet light and X-rays.

uranium—a dark gray metal, once considered useless, which is fuel for nuclear reactors. Uranium emits alpha rays.

X-rays—electromagnetic ionizing radiation of short wavelength that is capable of penetrating solid tissue.

Further Reading

This list of books and articles includes a range of opinion about the health risks of radiation, especially about low levels of ionizing radiation. To keep up-to-date with developments on this controversy, see especially: *Science, The Bulletin of the Atomic Scientists,* and *Technology Review.* In all periodicals, watch for follow-up letters that comment on published studies and opinions.

Chapman, J.M., and Ayrey, G. *The Use of Radioactive Isotopes in the Life Sciences.* Boston: Allen and Unwin, 1981.

Chester, Michael. *Particles: An Introduction to Particle Physics.* New York: Macmillan Publishing Co., Inc., 1978.

Committee for the Compilation of Materials on Damage Caused by the Atomic Bombs in Hiroshima and Nagasaki. *Hiroshima and Nagasaki: The Physical, Medical, and Social Effects of the Atomic Bombings.* New York: Basic Books, Inc., 1981.

Ecker, Martin, and Bramesco, Norton. *Radiation: All You Need to Know to Stop Worrying—Or to Start.* New York: Vintage Books, 1981.

Gofman, John. *Radiation and Human Health: A Comprehensive Investigation of the Evidence Relating Low-Level Radiation to Cancer and Other Diseases.* San Francisco: Sierra Club, 1981.

Gregg, E.C. "Radiation Risks with Diagnostic X-Rays." *Radiology,* Volume 123 (1977), pp. 447-453.

Jablon, S., and Miller, R.W. "Army Technologists: 29-Year Followup For Cause of Death." *Radiology,* Volume 126 (1978), pp. 677-679.

Marshall, Eliot. "Japanese A-Bomb Data Will Be Revised," *Science,* October 2, 1981, pp. 31-32.

Marshall, Eliot, "New A-Bomb Studies After Radiation Estimates." *Science,* May 22, 1981, pp. 900-903.

Marx, Jean. "Low-Level Radiation: Just How Bad Is It?" *Science,* April 13, 1979, pp. 160-164.

Moghossi, A.A., and Carter, M.W. *Public Health Implication of Radioluminous Materials.* U.S. Department of Health, Education, and Welfare Publication Number 76-8001, 1975.

Panati, Charles, and Hudson, Michael. *The Silent Intruder: Surviving the Radiation Age.* Boston: Houghton Mifflin Company, 1981.

Pringle, Laurence. *Nuclear Power: From Physics to Politics.* New York: Macmillan Publishing Co., Inc., 1979.

Pykett, Ian. "NMR Imaging in Medicine." *Scientific American,* May 1982, pp.78-88.

Radford, Edward. "Cancer Risks from Ionizing Radiation." *Technology Review,* November-December 1981, pp. 66-71, 76-78.

Robinson, Nathan, editor. *Solar Radiation.* New York: Elsevier Publishing Co., 1966.

Rotblat, Joseph. "Hazards of Low-Level Radiation—Less Agreement, More Confusion," *The Bulletin of the Atomic Scientists.* June-July 1981, pp. 31-36.

Shapiro, Fred. *Radwaste: A Reporter's Investigation of a Growing Nuclear Menace.* New York: Random House, 1981.

Shapiro, Jacob. *Radiation Protection: A Guide for Scientists and Physicians.* Cambridge, Mass.: Harvard University Press, 1981.

Shell, Ellen. "CAT Fever: A Questionable Prognosis." *Technology Review,* July 1981, pp. 23-26.

Skalnic, J.R. "Radiation Reduction." *Radiology Today,* December-January 1980, pp. 6-19.

Tabor, Martha. "Video Display Terminals: The Eyes Have Had It!" *Occupational Health and Safety,* September 1981, pp. 30-38.

Upton, Arthur. "The Biological Effects of Low-Level Ionizing Radiation." *Scientific American,* February 1982, pp. 41-49.

Index